ANCIENT
MAYA
INSIDE OUT

Rachel Stuckey

Crabtree Publishing Company
www.crabtreebooks.com

Author: Rachel Stuckey

Editors: Sarah Eason, Kelly Spence, Ellen Rodger, and Kathy Middleton

Editorial director: Kathy Middleton

Design: Paul Myerscough

Cover design: Paul Myerscough

Photo research: Rachel Blount

Proofreader: Wendy Scavuzzo

Production coordinator and Prepress technician: Tammy McGarr

Print coordinator: Margaret Amy Salter

Consultant: John Malam, archaeologist

Written and produced for Crabtree Publishing Company by Calcium Creative

Front Cover
BKGD: The ruins of Tikal, a powerful Maya city between 200 CE and 900 CE.
Inset: The funerary mask of the king of Palenque, a Maya city-state.
Title Page
BKGD: The ruins of Palenque.
Inset: A Maya sculpture which includes traces of cinnabar, a bright red mineral.

Photo Credits:

t=Top, bl=Bottom Left, br=Bottom Right

Alamy: Age Fotostock: p. 27t; Getty Images: Gilberto Villasana/ AFP: p. 17b; LACMA www.lacma.org: p. 19b, p. 21t; Gift of Constance McCormick Fearing (M.86.311.6): p. 1fg, p. 9b; Purchased with funds provided by Camilla Chandler Frost: p. 15b; Shutterstock: Subbotina Anna: p. 22–23; Anton_Ivanov: p. 1bg, Svetlana Bykova: p. 18–19; DC_Aperture: p. 4–5; Tami Freed: p. 3; Diego Grandi: p. 6–7; Ammit Jack: p. 14–15; Patryk Kosmider: p. 26–27; Jess Kraft: p. 10–11, p. 28–29; Tommaso Lizzul: p. 24–25; Stephen Marques: p. 5bc; Milosz Maslanka: p. 12–13; Matyas Rehak: p. 8–9; SL-Photography: p. 20–21; Jo Ann Snover: p. 16–17; Wikimedia Commons: Simon Burchell: p. 25b; Mariordo (Mario Roberto Durán Ortiz): p. 13t; Wolfgang Sauber: p. 11b; Unknown: p. 28br; Michel Wal (Own work): p. 23b.

Map p. 5 by Geoff Ward. Artwork p. 29 by Venetia Dean.

Cover: Shutterstock: Mark Yarchoan (bg); Wikimedia Commons: Wolfgang Sauber (br).

Library and Archives Canada Cataloguing in Publication

Stuckey, Rachel, author
    Ancient Maya inside out / Rachel Stuckey.

(Ancient worlds inside out)
Includes index.
Issued in print and electronic formats.
ISBN 978-0-7787-2878-8 (hardcover).--
ISBN 978-0-7787-2892-4 (softcover).--
ISBN 978-1-4271-1848-6 (HTML)

    1. Mayas--Social life and customs--Juvenile literature.
2. Mayas--Antiquities--Juvenile literature. 3. Mayas--Material culture--Juvenile literature. 4. Mayas--History--Juvenile literature. I. Title.

F1435.S885 2017   j972.81'016   C2016-907261-4
                                            C2016-907262-2

Library of Congress Cataloging-in-Publication Data

Names: Stuckey, Rachel, author.
Title: Ancient Maya inside out / Rachel Stuckey.
Description: New York : Crabtree Publishing Company, 2017. | Series: Ancient Worlds Inside Out | Includes index.
Identifiers: LCCN 2017001248 (print) | LCCN 2017002222 (ebook) ISBN 9780778728788 (reinforced library binding : alk. paper) | ISBN 9780778728924 (pbk. : alk. paper) | ISBN 9781427118486 (Electronic HTML)
Subjects: LCSH: Mayas--Juvenile literature. | Mexico--Civilization--Juvenile literature. | Central America--Civilization--Juvenile literature.
Classification: LCC F1435 .S895 2017 (print) | LCC F1435 (ebook) | DDC 972/.6--dc23
LC record available at https://lccn.loc.gov/2017001248

Crabtree Publishing Company
www.crabtreebooks.com   1-800-387-7650

Printed in Canada/032017/EF20170202

Published in Canada
Crabtree Publishing
616 Welland Ave.
St. Catharines, Ontario
L2M 5V6

Published in the United States
Crabtree Publishing
PMB 59051
350 Fifth Avenue, 59th Floor
New York, New York 10118

Published in the United Kingdom
Crabtree Publishing
Maritime House
Basin Road North, Hove
BN41 1WR

Published in Australia
Crabtree Publishing
3 Charles Street
Coburg North
VIC, 3058

CONTENTS

WHO WERE THE ANCIENT MAYA?

Thousands of years ago, the ancient Maya civilization thrived in **Mesoamerica**. The Maya are famous for their calendar, which followed the **solar year**. They had an advanced understanding of **astronomy**, gained from observing the Moon, stars, and planets in the sky. They built thousands of stone monuments and buildings and lived in **densely** populated cities. The Maya civilization thrived for more than 1,000 years before its mysterious decline.

Rise and Fall

The Maya civilization peaked between 250 C.E. and 900 C.E., with its population reaching about 2 million. After 950 C.E., the civilization started to collapse and the Maya abandoned many of their cities. When the Spanish **conquistadors** arrived in Mesoamerica in the 1520s, the Maya population had decreased. People had moved to smaller communities, and only a few great cities remained. Many abandoned Maya cities were overgrown with jungle plants.

Not an Empire

We often think the Maya are similar to the Aztec and Inca, two other Mesoamerican cultures. These civilizations were powerful **empires** that fought the Spanish conquistadors. But there was no Maya empire. The Maya were a cultural group that developed over thousands of years, and lived in hundreds of cities and villages in present-day southern Mexico, Guatemala, Belize, Honduras, and El Salvador. These Maya cities and villages shared many similarities. They were also unique in many ways, with their own languages, rituals, and artwork.

What Is an Ancient Civilization?

Large settlements of people formed the basis of the first civilizations. Through farming, these settlements grew into larger cities. Writing systems, social classes, and structured governments soon developed. These early settlements led to the later development of present-day cities, states, and countries.

The city of Tulum was one of the last great Maya cities.

Key

The Maya cultural area

Present-day borders

Chichén Itzá

Tulum

Gulf of Mexico

This map shows the main sites of the Maya civilization.

Palenque

Mexico

Belize

Caribbean Sea

Guatemala

Honduras

Pacific Ocean

El Salvador

DIGGING UP THE PAST

One hundred years ago, archaeologists believed the Maya civilization began around 300 C.E. More recent discoveries reveal that the Maya started building cities as early as 600 B.C.E., or 900 years earlier. With each new discovery, archaeologists must update their theories about the Maya civilization.

Maya Primary Sources

Archaeologists have learned about the Maya from many different sources. The great stone cities built by the Maya include pyramids, temples, palaces, ball courts, and large monuments known as **stelae**. All of these structures feature carvings, inscriptions, and paintings. Archaeologists have discovered jewelry, sculptures, painted pottery, and books written by the Maya called codices. Maya paintings often show scenes of everyday life. This reveals information about what the Maya wore and what foods they ate. There are two important discoveries that have helped us learn the most about the Maya. First, **linguists** learned how to **translate** the Maya writing system. This helped archaeologists understand the carvings, inscriptions, paintings, and codices. Then, by decoding the Maya calendar, archaeologists could use our own calendar to figure out when events occurred or when monuments were built.

Maya Timeline

Archaeologists use three main periods to identify different parts of Maya civilization. The Pre-Classic Era lasted from around 1800 B.C.E. to 250 C.E. The Classic Era was from 250 C.E. to 900 C.E.—the height of the civilization. The Post-Classic Era lasted from 900 C.E. until the Spanish conquest in the mid-1500s.

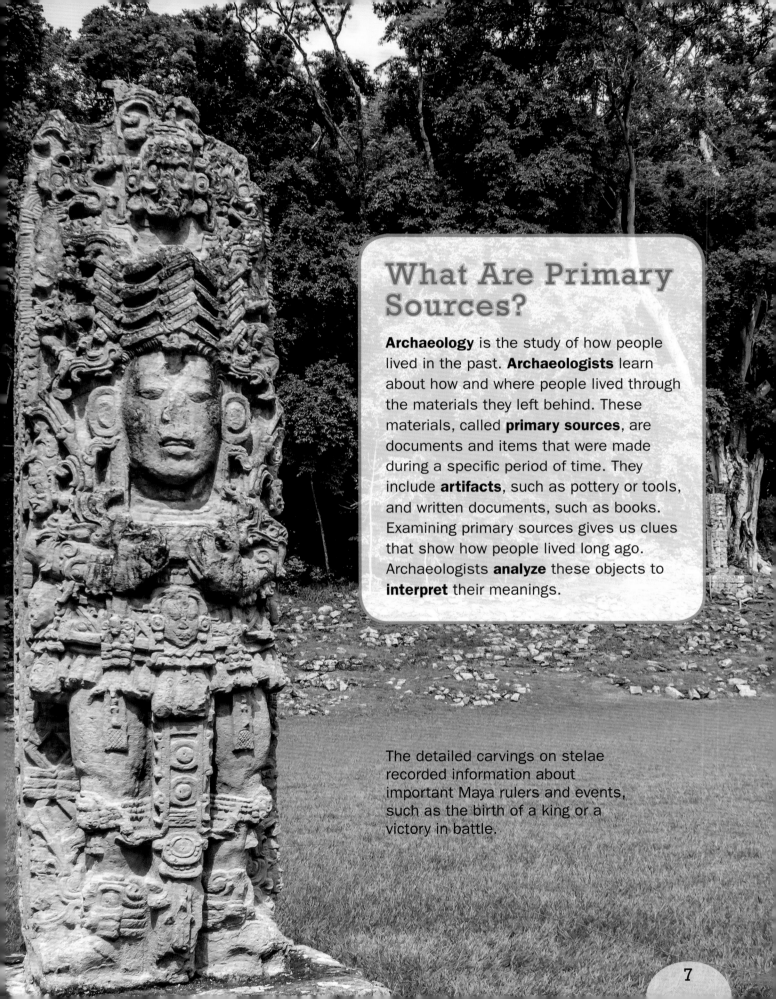

What Are Primary Sources?

Archaeology is the study of how people lived in the past. **Archaeologists** learn about how and where people lived through the materials they left behind. These materials, called **primary sources**, are documents and items that were made during a specific period of time. They include **artifacts**, such as pottery or tools, and written documents, such as books. Examining primary sources gives us clues that show how people lived long ago. Archaeologists **analyze** these objects to **interpret** their meanings.

The detailed carvings on stelae recorded information about important Maya rulers and events, such as the birth of a king or a victory in battle.

MESOAMERICA

Together, the **indigenous** cultures of southern Mexico and Central America are called Mesoamerican. *Meso* means "in the middle"— and Central America is a narrow piece of land that links together North America and South America. The ancient peoples who lived in the area before the Spanish arrived, and their descendants who live there today, are the Mesoamerican peoples.

The mountains of Mesoamerica formed natural barriers between Maya cities.

The Maya Cultural Area

The Maya were one of the largest ancient cultures in Mesoamerica. They were spread out over a large territory with many different landscapes. The Maya cultural area was surrounded by water on three sides: the Gulf of Mexico, the Caribbean Sea, and the Pacific Ocean. The area covered more than 150,000 square miles (389,000 sq km)—or most of modern-day Central America, including the Yucatan Peninsula and part of Southern Mexico. The Maya lived in many different environments. The Yucatan Peninsula has tropical lowlands surrounded by the seas. The Maya also lived in the highlands, which were cold and dry, and even had snow-capped mountains and volcanoes.

Maya Isolation

The lands of the Maya were very **fertile**, thanks to tropical rain forests in the lowlands and volcanic ash in the highlands. The Maya traded with other cultures. But the mountains and difficult terrain to the north and south made it difficult for new peoples to travel to the region, and for the Maya to leave their cultural area.

History Up Close

The Olmec peoples lived in Mexico between 1200 and 400 B.C.E. The Maya civilization first emerged as the Olmec disappeared. This Olmec figurine is made of serpentine, a dark green stone which often looks like snake skin. The sculpture has the features of both a human and a jaguar. The missing eye stones were probably made of pyrite, a shiny yellow mineral. This would have made the eyes appear to glow—like those of a jaguar. The Olmec culture influenced all of the Mesoamerican cultures that came after it.

Olmec figurine

MAYA GOVERNMENTS

There were hundreds of cities and smaller settlements located throughout the Maya cultural area. Some cities were more important than others. Archaeologists believe that different cities rose to power at different times. No single city ever ruled over all the Maya people. Smaller cities may have depended on larger cities nearby, creating small **chiefdoms**, but archaeologists do not know this for sure.

Royal Rulers

Each Maya city was ruled by a king, called an *ahau*. The Maya worshiped their ancestors, so royal **dynasties**—the king and his ancestors—were very important. The people worshiped their rulers like gods. They were also very loyal to their rulers. The Maya depended on storing food and water for the dry season and the rulers controlled these resources. The rulers were also priests who performed important religious rituals known only to the ruling class.

Growing Equality

For a long time, archaeologists believed that Maya kings were all powerful and that society was strictly divided. The **elite** or ruling class made up around 10 percent of the population. Known as the *itz'at winik,* or "wise people," the elites could read and write and were very wealthy. But new evidence shows that the Maya did have organized governments, with officials who worked on behalf of the kings. Archaeologists also think that Maya society became less rigid over time. As the society grew in size and people learned to grow more food, some people could move from farming to other trades. As wealth increased, the common people did not rely on the elite. Social positions also became less strict. But only the elite could become priests and perform religious rituals.

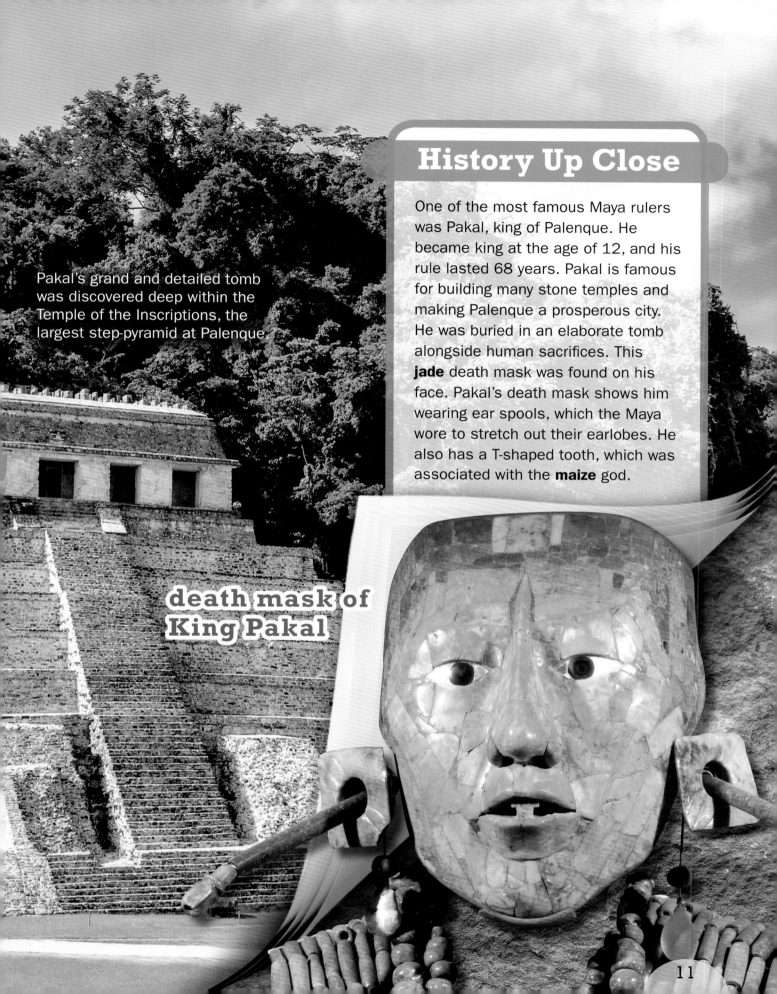

Pakal's grand and detailed tomb was discovered deep within the Temple of the Inscriptions, the largest step-pyramid at Palenque.

History Up Close

One of the most famous Maya rulers was Pakal, king of Palenque. He became king at the age of 12, and his rule lasted 68 years. Pakal is famous for building many stone temples and making Palenque a prosperous city. He was buried in an elaborate tomb alongside human sacrifices. This **jade** death mask was found on his face. Pakal's death mask shows him wearing ear spools, which the Maya wore to stretch out their earlobes. He also has a T-shaped tooth, which was associated with the **maize** god.

death mask of King Pakal

EVERYDAY PEOPLE

Maya society was strictly divided between the elite and the ordinary people, or commoners. Archaeologists do not know very much about the life of commoners—most artifacts and texts describe the elite class. But we do know there was a clear divide between women and men.

The Maya Family

The Maya families lived in **compounds** made up of many buildings. Families were large and children were educated at home and learned skills from their parents. The Maya considered a flat, sloped forehead to be attractive. Parents tied boards to their children's foreheads while they were young, so their skulls would grow that way. Teenage boys lived in shared dorms, and teenage girls lived at home. Before they could marry, young people went through rituals in which they were recognized as adults. Marriages were arranged, but couples could get divorced and remarry. After marriage, a young couple lived in the wife's family compound. After a few years, they built a home on the husband's family land. Sons inherited from their fathers. Daughters inherited nothing.

The Common People

Most Maya were ordinary workers and farmers. They are not described in Maya texts or included in Maya artwork. The Maya elite needed farmers to grow food and laborers to build the temples. The elite also needed servants. Commoners were not allowed to wear fancy clothes and jewelry like the elite—even if they could afford them. There was also a small middle class of merchants and government officials. While the middle class could earn great wealth, they could never join the elite, who **inherited** their status from their parents. The Maya also had slaves, who were often prisoners from rival cities. Criminals were also sometimes forced to become slaves as punishment for their crimes.

Eighteen buildings have been unearthed at Joya de Cerén, including houses, storehouses, a kitchen, and a **sauna**.

bowl

History Up Close

Around 590 C.E., a volcano erupted in what is now southwest El Salvador. The people in a nearby village escaped. But their homes, furniture, and possessions were buried under 16 feet (5 m) of volcanic ash. The site, known today as Joya de Cerén, was discovered in the 1970s. This decorated ceramic bowl was found there, well preserved beneath the ash. The discoveries of luxurious items such as this bowl and jade axes have changed archaeologists' understanding of ancient Maya society. These artifacts show that people who lived in a farming village could own expensive items, which they would have received through trade with the elite class.

Dig Deeper!

Most of our knowledge about the Maya comes from stone monuments and inscriptions about the kings, priests, and elite class. What new information can archaeologists learn from a site such as Joya de Cerén?

FOOD AND FARMING

The people of Mesoamerica learned to grow maize, what we call corn, between 3000 and 2000 B.C.E. Mesoamerican civilizations, including the Maya, depended on corn. Archaeologists believe that about 90 percent of the Maya population were farmers.

What Did the Maya Eat?

By testing ancient skeletons, scientists have learned that the Maya had a very healthy diet. Corn was the most important food. The Maya also grew squash, pumpkins, tomatoes, peppers, nuts, and fruits. They also kept bees to make honey. Depending on where they lived, the Maya ate venison (deer), turkey, and shellfish. Corn was used to make tamales—steamed corn dough stuffed with meat or beans. The Maya also ate a corn gruel called **atole**. The elite mixed it with chocolate, and commoners added chili peppers, pumpkin seeds, honey, and herbs. Maya workers carried hollowed-out gourds filled with atole for their lunch. The Maya also made a corn drink called *chicha*.

Chocolate Lovers

Maya chocolate was not like the chocolate people enjoy today—they did not add sugar or milk. The Maya toasted cacao beans, then ground them to make a hot drink. They also added it to other foods, such as sauces, and made cacao butter. Cacao beans were a chief crop for the Maya. The beans were also used for trade and were very valuable. Cacao beans could not be stored—they had to be used right after the harvest.

14

Cacao beans grow inside large pods. Each pod contains between 20 and 60 beans.

History Up Close

Cacao was an important part of the Maya culture and diet. This cup is from 700–850 c.e. and was found in Petén, Guatemala. In the painting, a lord is holding his hand above a pot of a cacao drink his servant has brought him. The foam on top of the drink was made by pouring the liquid from one bowl into another. There is also a bowl of tamales with a dark sauce that is probably made from chilies and cacao. Many cups contain inscriptions that reveal they were made for drinking cacao.

cacao vessel

Dig Deeper!

The lord painted on the cup is shown with a pot of drinking chocolate. Why do you think this might have been a symbol of his importance or wealth?

SCIENCE AND TECHNOLOGY

The Maya are famous for their calendar and their advanced understanding of astronomy and mathematics.

Looking to the Skies

The Maya mapped the phases of the Moon and planets, and created detailed charts that showed the cycles of the night sky. The movement of Venus was important to the Maya. Charts showing the planet's cycle are found in the codices. Maya **oral history** tells us that they may be the only civilization without telescopes to discover that Orion was a **nebula**, not just a single star. Many Maya temples and other buildings line up with celestial events, such as an **equinox**, so that light shines in a certain way, or stars and planets can be seen through windows and doorways.

Measuring Time

The Maya calendar has two main parts: the *Tzolk'in* and the *Haab'*. The *Tzolk'in* is a 260-day sacred cycle made up of 13 months of 20 days. Each day has its own name. The *Haab'* is the 365-day cycle based on the solar year—it has 18 months of 20 days. The Maya knew the solar year was not exact, so they added five extra days called the *Wayeb*. The *Tzolk'in* and *Haab'* cycles overlapped, and it took 52 years for them to begin again at the same starting point. This is known as the Calendar Round. The Long Count is a separate system used to measure lengths of time that are longer than 52 years. It measures time in five cycles from a starting date of August 11, 3114 B.C.E. That is the day the Maya believed the world was created.

Counting System

The Maya had a simple number system that allowed them to express large numbers. Archaeologists have found inscriptions with numbers well over a million. The Maya also understood the concept of zero, which they represented with a shell. They used a base-20 system. This means they counted by 20 before going to the next level—the way we count to 10.

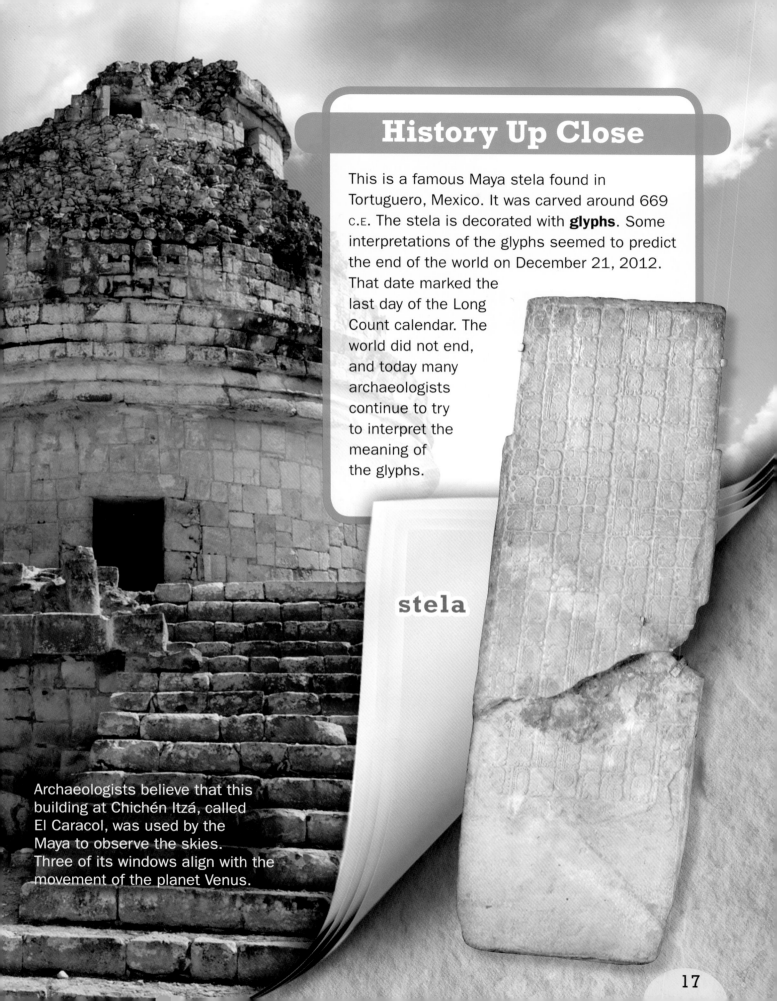

This is a famous Maya stela found in Tortuguero, Mexico. It was carved around 669 c.e. The stela is decorated with **glyphs**. Some interpretations of the glyphs seemed to predict the end of the world on December 21, 2012. That date marked the last day of the Long Count calendar. The world did not end, and today many archaeologists continue to try to interpret the meaning of the glyphs.

stela

Archaeologists believe that this building at Chichén Itzá, called El Caracol, was used by the Maya to observe the skies. Three of its windows align with the movement of the planet Venus.

THE MAYA BUILDERS

Maya architecture went through many changes over 2,000 years—from simple burial mounds to great stone pyramids. They also built palaces, ball courts, tombs, and stone monuments called stelae.

Step by Step

Maya pyramids are called **step pyramids**. They have **terraces**, or flat platforms, on each level, and stairways. Each pyramid was dedicated to a god and had a shrine or temple at the top. The Maya also built round temples. Today, these structures are often called **observatories** because they look similar to modern-day observatories. However, there is no evidence that these buildings were used only for astronomy. Stone ball courts are found near most temples and palaces—they are shaped like a capital I, with sloped walls. The ball game was very important in Mesoamerica. To play, teams passed a rubber ball using their hips, and shot it through a stone ring high on the wall.

Engineering and Building Methods

The Maya built their stone cities with materials that were found nearby, such as limestone. The heavy stones were often transported on large rollers to the building site, where builders shaped limestone with stone and wooden tools. They sometimes used **mortar**, but they also learned to shape stones to fit together without any mortar.

The White Way

In some parts of the Maya cultural area, **causeways** were built. These long, white limestone roads were called *sacbeob* by the Maya, meaning "the white way." A sacbe connecting Cobá and Yaxuna, two cities on the Yucatan Peninsula, measures 62 miles (100 km) in length.

In the city of Tikal, archaeologists have found ruins of structures that were built at different times during a period of about 1,500 years.

History Up Close

Maya censers were freestanding sculptures that were often placed in temples. A brazier, a bowl for burning **incense**, would have been placed on top. This censer is decorated with human and animal figures that represent the Sun gods worshiped by the Maya. The censer was made of clay, then fired like pottery and painted blue. Some of the paint still remains. Censers were some of the most sophisticated sculptures created by Maya artists. This censer is from the late Classic period and was found near the ruins of Palenque in present-day Chiapas, Mexico.

censer

LANGUAGE AND LITERATURE

The Maya are famous for having a written language, but most people were not able to read and write. Archaeologists are not sure if all of the elite could read and write. We know that some elite women could read and write because there are paintings of female scribes.

Mayan Language

People spoke different languages in different parts of the Maya cultural area. The languages were related, but speakers of different Mayan languages could not understand each other. The Spanish reported more than 30 different Mayan languages in the 1500s. However, Maya scholars think that the Maya elite may have had a shared royal **dialect** upon which the writing system was based.

Maya Writing

The Maya created the only system in the ancient **Americas** that represented their entire spoken language. The system had more than 1,000 glyphs and combined **hieroglyphics**, or a system of writing using pictures, and **phonetic** symbols. Archaeologists have found more than 10,000 texts. These are mostly inscriptions in stone and on pottery. We know the Maya also used ink and brushes or quill pens to write on a paper-like material made from tree bark. They even created a type of folding book called a **codex** that recorded their history, religion, and culture.

The Codices and the Conquest

Four Maya codices have been found. They codices were written hundreds of years before the Spanish conquest and contain astronomical and mathematical information. Unfortunately, most of the codices and other documents were destroyed during the conquest. After the conquest, the Maya started using the **Roman alphabet** to write documents in Mayan languages. They kept these documents a secret from the Spanish. One example of this is the famous *Popol Vuh*, which tells the history of the Quiche people and the Maya story of creation.

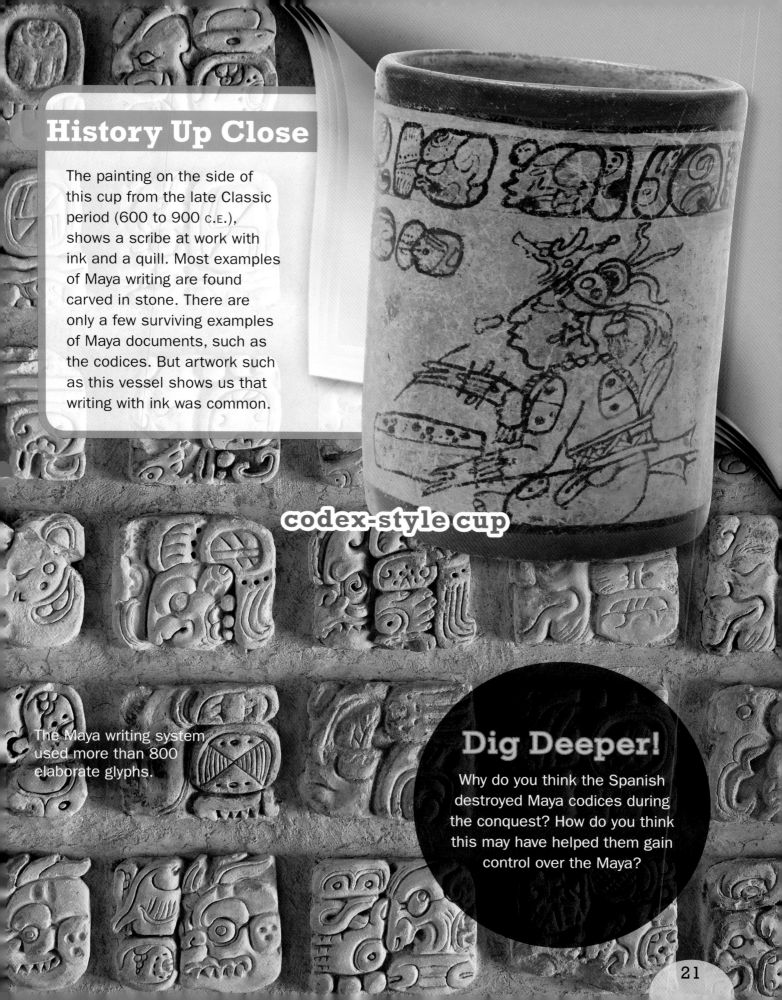

History Up Close

The painting on the side of this cup from the late Classic period (600 to 900 C.E.), shows a scribe at work with ink and a quill. Most examples of Maya writing are found carved in stone. There are only a few surviving examples of Maya documents, such as the codices. But artwork such as this vessel shows us that writing with ink was common.

codex-style cup

The Maya writing system used more than 800 elaborate glyphs.

Dig Deeper!

Why do you think the Spanish destroyed Maya codices during the conquest? How do you think this may have helped them gain control over the Maya?

GODS AND THE AFTERLIFE

There were hundreds of Maya gods with many different identities, such as the Moon god or the maize god. Itzamna was the creator god and K'inich Ahau was the Sun god. The Maya also believed their kings were **divine**, and that they became gods when they died.

The Maya and Nature

The natural world was an important part of the Maya belief system. In artwork, gods take the form of snakes, monkeys, jaguars, crocodiles, and other creatures. The Maya also believed in the cyclical nature of time. They used their calendar to track the changing seasons and the movement of the planets. The cycle of time was also the cycle of life. The dry season brought the end of a growing cycle, and the rainy season brought everything back to life.

Human Sacrifice

Human sacrifice is the ritual or ceremonial killing of a person to honor the gods. This was common in the ancient civilizations of Mesoamerica. The Maya saw the natural world as a cycle of life and death. To the Maya, death eventually brought life again, so sacrificing people to the gods would also bring new life. Prisoners, slaves, and children were often sacrificed in ceremonies. Sometimes sacrifices were made to the gods by throwing a person into a **cenote**, a deep sinkhole filled with water.

The Universe

To the Maya, the universe was flat, but **infinite**. There were three levels: the underworld, the sky, and the earth. The Maya believed that caves and other holes or passageways were entrances to the underworld, where the dead were said to meet the death gods.

The Maya believed that blood provided food for the gods. Rulers sometimes cut their own bodies to offer their blood as a sacrifice, and to communicate with their ancestors. This was called **bloodletting**. This carved **lintel**, which dates from 723–726 C.E., shows a bloodletting ceremony. Shield Jaguar II, king of Yaxchilan, waves a torch above his wife, Lady K'ab'al Xook. Her tongue is pierced by a spiked rope. Blood is shown dripping from her mouth onto paper below. After the ceremony, the paper would have been burned to carry the blood to the gods. The glyphs along the top of the lintel reveal that the ceremony took place in 709 C.E. in Yaxchilan.

lintel

Humans were sacrificed to the rain god Chaak in water-filled sinkholes such as this one located near the ruins of Chichén Itzá.

TRADE AND WARFARE

While the great stone cities built by the Maya were never united under a single ruler, the separate cities and villages still had contact with each other. Trade thrived between inland cities and those on the coast. At times, cities went to war with one another to gain control of more territory and riches.

Trade Goods and Routes

The Maya did not use coins or paper money. Instead, they traded goods, such as cacao, obsidian (a black glassy, volcanic rock), salt, feathers, jade, and gold. In areas along the coast, seawater was collected and dried on large, flat surfaces. The remaining salt was then collected and transported inland. Obsidian and jade were mined in quarries in the highlands of Guatemala. Over time, trade across water routes became more common, especially along the Yucatan Peninsula. Large canoes were used to carry goods up and down the coast, and along rivers to inland settlements. Boats were made from hollowed-out tree trunks and had curved ends.

Battles Between Maya Cities

For many years, archaeologists believed that the Maya had been a peaceful civilization. But a closer examination of artwork and archaeological sites revealed that warfare was common, particularly during the Post-Classic period (1000–1521 c.e.). The most famous battle recorded by the Maya lasted more than 200 years. It was fought between Calakmul, in modern-day Belize, and Tikal. Eventually, Calakmul joined forces with the city of Caracol, and defeated Tikal in 562 c.e. Some scholars believe that wars were fought to capture prisoners that could be sacrificed to the gods, and also to control resources, such as food. Maya history also tells about bloody battles called "star wars." These were fought during specific times of the year, based on Venus's movements in the sky.

Between 1200 and 400 C.E., the coastal city of Tulum on the Yucatan Peninsula was an important trading **port** for the ancient Maya.

History Up Close

Obsidian is found in the highlands of Central America. These obsidian spearheads were discovered in Palenque and date from the Late Classic period (600–900 C.E.). Obsidian was used to make axes, mirrors, and many other tools. Archaeologists are able to identify where obsidian used to make these items came from. This information can be used to map trade routes used by the ancient Maya.

obsidian spearheads

THE DECLINE OF THE MAYA

Early explorers believed the ancient Maya simply mysteriously disappeared. However, we know now that around 950 c.e., the Maya started to move out of their great cities as their numbers began to decrease. They continued to live in the Yucatan Peninsula and the Guatemalan highlands for hundreds of years, and many survived the Spanish conquest. Today, there are more than 7 million people in Central America who speak Mayan languages.

The Decline of the Maya

There are many theories about why the Maya civilization declined after 900 c.e. The decline was probably caused by many related events that took place over hundreds of years. However, there is evidence in satellite photos of historic **deforestation** and **drought**. This would have caused a food shortage, leading the Maya to abandon some of their inland cities. There is archaeological evidence in some cities of warfare and a revolt led by the commoners against the elite, both of which were likely caused by famine. The forest has grown back now, but evidence shows that the ancient Maya cut down all the trees—probably for building materials, fuel, and to create farmland.

The Spanish Conquest

Even as the population declined, the Maya continued to live in cities along the coast, such as Chichén Itzá, until the Spanish arrived in 1519. Conquistador Hernán Cortés overthrew the coastal Maya cities on the Yucatan Peninsula. Then he moved north to conquer the Aztec Empire. Many Maya cities were able to resist the Spanish for a while—especially those located deep in the jungle. It took more than 150 years for the Spanish to conquer all of the Maya peoples.

New Discoveries

For hundreds of years, people have come up with theories about the Maya. However, as new evidence was discovered, their theories changed. Our understanding of this fascinating civilization continues to grow. Archaeological work continues in Mesoamerica today. Every year, millions of tourists visit Maya ruins all over Mexico and Central America such as Tulum, Chichén Itzá, Tikal, and Copán. These sites are also working archaeological digs. Much remains to be discovered about the Maya.

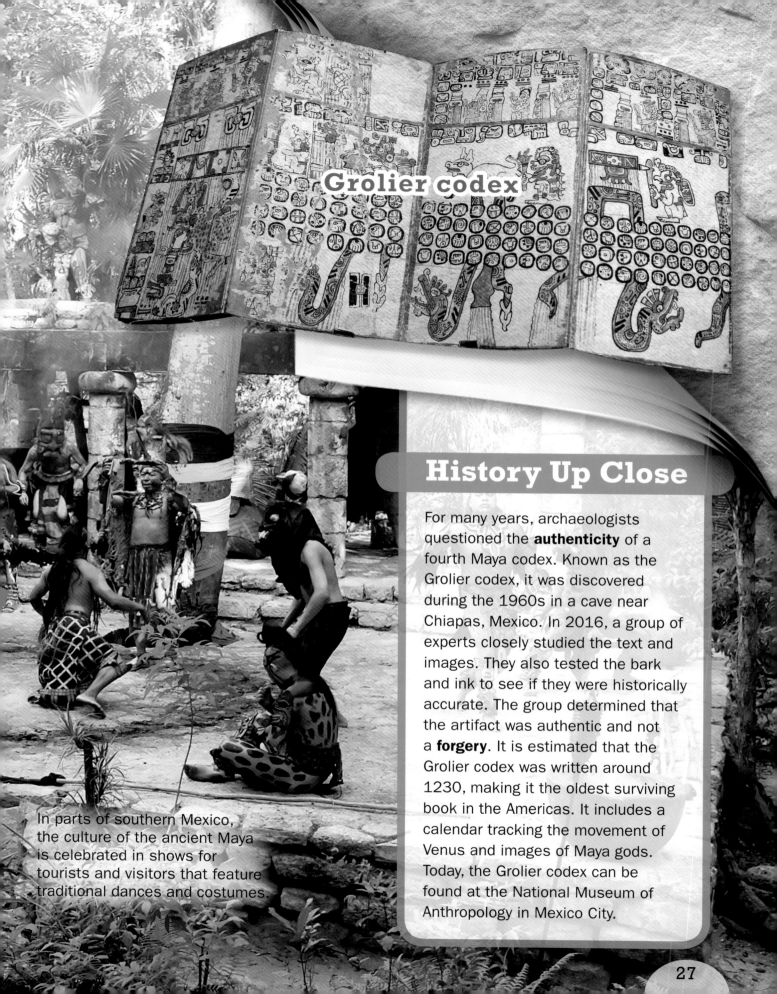

Grolier codex

History Up Close

For many years, archaeologists questioned the **authenticity** of a fourth Maya codex. Known as the Grolier codex, it was discovered during the 1960s in a cave near Chiapas, Mexico. In 2016, a group of experts closely studied the text and images. They also tested the bark and ink to see if they were historically accurate. The group determined that the artifact was authentic and not a **forgery**. It is estimated that the Grolier codex was written around 1230, making it the oldest surviving book in the Americas. It includes a calendar tracking the movement of Venus and images of Maya gods. Today, the Grolier codex can be found at the National Museum of Anthropology in Mexico City.

In parts of southern Mexico, the culture of the ancient Maya is celebrated in shows for tourists and visitors that feature traditional dances and costumes.

COUNT LIKE THE MAYA

The Maya created a math system that allowed everyday people to perform simple calculations. The system was also used to represent large numbers using dots, lines, and shells. Understanding the Maya number system has helped archaeologists read Maya texts such as the codices, and monuments such as stelae. The Maya are also the first known culture in the Americas to discover the importance of 0.

The Maya System

The Maya used place value to show large numbers. Place value is the value a digit has based on its position in a whole number. The Maya system counted by 20s instead of 10s, the system that is common today. In the Maya number system, a pebble represents 1, a stick represents 5, and a shell represents 0. The chart below shows the Maya counting system from 0–19.

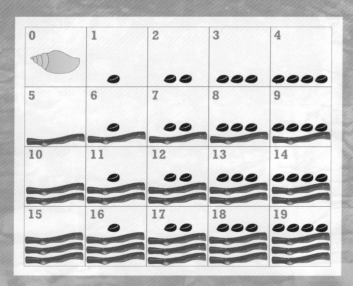

The dots and lines on this codex page represent dates.

28

Activity:

Maya Math

Practice showing numbers with the Maya number system.

You Will Need:

- Poster board
- Black marker
- Ruler
- Small stones, sticks, and shells
- A partner
- A calculator

Instructions

A grid is a helpful tool to show the different values in larger numbers. Use a ruler and a black marker to divide the poster board into columns. Each column should have two squares. Write a 1 beside the bottom row of squares and write a 20 beside the top row. Collect some stones, sticks, and shells.

The Challenge

With a partner, practice showing numbers on the grid using the Maya system illustrated on page 28. Look at examples A and B shown below. Remember, to show a number greater than 19, you must move to the top row. This is because the Maya system counted by 20s instead of 10s, and the number in the top row must be multiplied by 20 to calculate its value. That value is then added to the bottom number to show the whole number represented by that column.

Once you have mastered showing numbers on the grid, you and your partner can work together to add and subtract numbers. What equations can you create? What is the highest number you can reach?

How effective do you think this number system would be for everyday people to learn? What are some of the benefits? What are some of the challenges?

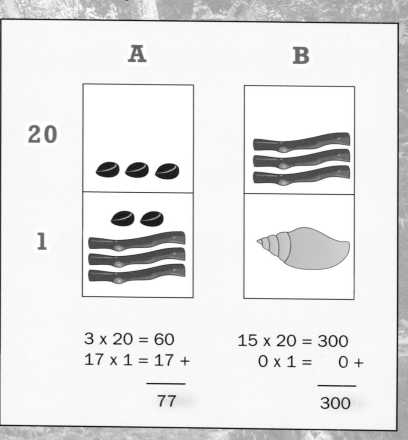

A

B

20

1

3 x 20 = 60
17 x 1 = 17 +
_____
77

15 x 20 = 300
0 x 1 = 0 +
_____
300

GLOSSARY

Note: Some bold-faced words are defined where they appear in the text.

Americas The area made up of North, South, and Central America

analyze To examine

artifacts Objects created by humans

astronomy The study of celestial bodies

atole A thin liquid made by boiling corn in milk or water

authenticity How genuine or real something is

bloodletting Cutting the body to draw blood

causeways Raised roadways

chiefdoms Small political groups made up of many villages or towns ruled over by a chief

codex A handwritten book made from attaching pages made from bark, paper

compounds Groups of shared buildings

conquistadors Spanish explorers and soldiers who conquered the New World

deforestation Cutting down all the trees in one area

densely Heavily; very crowded

dialect A variation of a language with some unique characteristics

divine Godlike

drought A period of dry weather that lasts a long time

dynasties Successions of rulers from the same family

elite People with wealth and social status

empires Groups of states controlled by a single ruler

equinox A time in the year when the Sun crosses the equator (an imaginary line around the center of the Earth) and day and night are of equal length

fertile Able to produce lots of vegetation, such as fruits, grains, and vegetables

forgery A fake copy

glyphs Pictures that represent words and ideas

incense A material, such as a spice, that produces a fragrance when burned

indigenous Native to an area

infinite Never-ending

interpret To figure out the meaning

inherited Gained or received something from a relative, often after that person has died

jade A hard green stone that is often carved

linguists People who study languages and how they work

lintel A horizontal support across a window or door

maize Corn; a type of grain native to Mesoamerica and widely grown by the Maya as a food crop

Mesoamerica The region in Central America where the Olmec, Maya, and Aztec lived

mortar A building material made of stone and liquid that hardens when it dries to keep stones or bricks together

nebula A cloud in space made up of gas and dust

observatories Places where people observe the night sky

oral history A history passed down through stories from one generation to the next

phonetic How words sound

port A town with a harbor where goods are loaded and unloaded for trade

Roman alphabet The same alphabet we use to write

sauna A room that is heated to make people sweat

scribes People who copy documents

solar year The amount of time it takes for a planet to revolve around the Sun

stelae (singular: stela) Carved stone pillars that are meant to remember an event or person

step pyramids Pyramids on which each level has a step or terrace

translate To change words from one language to another

Learning More

Want to learn more about the ancient Maya? Check out these resources.

Books

DK Publishing. *Aztec, Inca & Maya*. DK Publishing, 2011.

Harris, Nathaniel. *Ancient Maya: Archaeology Unlocks the Secrets of the Maya's Past*. National Geographic Children's Books, 2008.

Hunter, Nick. *Daily Life in the Maya Civilization*. Heinemann, 2015.

Hyde, Natalie. *Understanding Mesoamerican Myths*. Crabtree Publishing, 2012.

Pipe, Jim. *Mysteries of the Mayan Calendar*. Crabtree Publishing, 2012.

Spilsbury, Louise. *The Mayans*. Heinemann, 2016.

Websites

The Canadian Museum of History hosts an online exhibit on the fascinating culture of the Maya.
www.historymuseum.ca/cmc/exhibitions/civil/maya/mmc01eng.shtml

Explore the Maya calendar on this site from the Smithsonian National Museum of the American Indian.
http://maya.nmai.si.edu/calendar

The National Gallery of Art's publication *Courtly Art of the Ancient Maya* provides readers with information about artifacts from this fascinating Mesoamerican culture.
www.nga.gov/kids/mayakids.pdf

The Belize Institute of Archaeology presents a comprehensive overview of the Maya culture.
www.nichbelize.org/ia-archaeology/archaeology-in-belize.html

At this site from PBS, decode the hieroglyphs on a stela found in Piedras Negras in northwestern Guatemala.
www.pbs.org/wgbh/nova/ancient/decode-stela-3.html

Explore 15 ancient Maya archaeological sites on this interactive map.
www.pbs.org/wgbh/nova/ancient/map-of-the-maya-world.html

INDEX

ABOUT THE AUTHOR

Rachel Stuckey is a "digital nomad" freelance writer and editor based in Toronto, Canada. She has worked in educational publishing for more than a decade, and now focuses her creative energies on travel writing and books for young readers. She has written more than 20 books for children on a wide range of topics, and is currently working on a series of travel guides. Learn more at www.rachelstuckey.com and www.thenomadiceditor.com.